Contents

KU-769-268

What is Gymnastics?

Gymnastics is a sport of leaps, spins, flips and twists. Using special equipment, gymnasts can fly high enough to be able to leap over a van, or far enough to clear the length of a car from the bonnet to the boot!

Gymnastics in the Past

Gymnastics has been around for a very long time. Seven thousand years ago, female gymnasts performed routines for the pharaohs, the rulers of ancient Egypt. Through the ages, gymnasts have often earned a living by entertaining people. They were known as 'tumblers', and performed in travelling troupes or circuses.

Gymnastics has been a competitive sport for more than a hundred years. For example, there were gymnastics competitions at the first modern Olympics, which were held in 1896.

Modern Gymnastics

Today, most gymnasts train to take part in competitions. The sport is very popular with spectators. The gymnastics halls at the Olympics or the world championships are always crowded with fans, and major competitions are shown on T.V. all round the world.

2004 Olympic gold medalist, Paul Hamm of the USA, competes in the pommel horse section during the 2007 Visa Gymnastics Championship in San Jose, California.

OUR SPORT

Gymnastics

Paul Mason

W

FRANKLIN WATTS

LONDON • SYDNEY

First published in 2008 by
Franklin Watts
338 Euston Road
London NW1 3BH

Franklin Watts Australia
Hachette Children's Books
Level 17/207 Kent Street
Sydney NSW 2000

Series editor: Jeremy Smith
Art director: Jonathan Hair

Series designed and created for
Franklin Watts by Painted Fish Ltd.
Designer: Rita Storey
Editor: Nicola Edwards
Photography: Tudor Photography,
   Banbury

A CIP catalogue record
for this book is available
from the British Library.

Dewey classification: 796
ISBN: 978 0 7496 7838 8
Printed in China

Franklin Watts is a division of Hachette
Children's Books, an Hachette Livre UK
company.

Note: At the time of going to press, the statistics and player profiles in this book were up to date. However, due to some players' active participation in the sport, it is possible that some of these may now be out of date.

Picture credits
Martin Lauricella/Alamy p17, Bettmann/√ Corbis pp 15 and 27; istock p 22; Getty Images pp 6 and 23.

Cover images: Tudor Photography, Banbury.

All photos posed by models.
Thanks to Dené, Mel Furey, Andy Hall, Jessica Hall and Matt Moutos.

The Publisher would like to thank the Wade Gymnastics Club for all their help.

Warning!

Gymnastics is a dangerous sport, and can cause severe injuries such as **paralysis**. This book is not a self-teaching guide. Only ever learn gymnastics with a qualified coach.

Having a coach is vital for anyone who wants to improve their gymnastics. Coaches give advice on technique and fitness, as well as making sure that all the practices are done as safely as possible.

Types of Gymnastics

In competitions, gymnastics is divided into three separate categories: artistic gymnastics; rhythmic gymnastics and trampolining.

Artistic gymnastics is what most people think of when they hear someone talking about 'gymnastics'. Artistic gymnastics includes:

- For men: floor exercises, horizontal bar, parallel bars, pommel horse, rings and vault;

- For women: balance beam, floor exercises, uneven bars and vault.

This book is mostly about artistic gymnastics.

Judging and Scoring

Each time a gymnast completes a skill or routine in a competition, he or she is given a score. The scores are decided by a group of judges. Each judge awards a score based on difficulty and how well the routine has been performed. The highest and lowest scores are ignored, and the gymnast is awarded the average of the remaining scores. The highest possible score is 10.

Perfect 10

In 1976, Nadia Comaneci became the first gymnast to score a perfect 10 at the Olympics. She scored a total of seven 10s at the 1976 Games.

Gymnastics Basics

At the gym there is a wide variety of apparatus. Each piece of apparatus is used for different kinds of gymnastics. Apart from the apparatus, gymnasts do not need very much equipment. They use handguards and chalk to help them grip during some exercises, for example while swinging on the bars.

Clothing (males and females)

Most beginner gymnasts wear shorts and a gym vest, plus gym slippers. Once gymnasts become more experienced, female gymnasts usually wear a leotard. Male gymnasts wear either shorts or longer trousers, plus a gym vest. Tight-fitting, specially made gymnastics shoes give good grip and flexibility. A tracksuit is also useful, for keeping warm between exercises.

The Apparatus (males and females)

There are eight major pieces of equipment in a gymnastics competition. Some of these are used both by male and female gymnasts, others are used only by males or females. There are six events for male gymnasts, and four for females. Most gymnasts enter every event, which gives them a chance to win an overall artistic category medal. Some specialists enter just one or two events, such as parallel bars or vault, and aim only to win a medal in that specific event.

The Floor Area (males and females)

Gymnasts perform tumbling and

◄ These young gymnasts are wearing a mixture of clothing. The most important thing for beginners is that their clothes are not loose and flappy, so that they don't get in the way. ►

balance skills. Females perform a routine that can last up to 90 seconds, with music playing in the background. Males perform for 70 seconds and without music.

The Horizontal Bar (males only)

Gymnasts spin round and round the bar, sometimes letting go, changing their grip or twisting to add difficulty to their routine.

The Pommel Horse (males only)

The pommel horse has handles on top for the gymnast to hold on to. Male gymnasts hold on to the handles and perform routines based on swinging their body and legs around the horse.

The Rings (males only)

Male gymnasts hang from the rings forming special shapes, for example a cross-shape, with their body. During the routine they must try to keep the rings – which hang from cables – as still as possible.

The Parallel Bars (males only)

Only male gymnasts use the parallel bars (see pages 18-19). They perform handstands, swings, twists and other movements.

The Vaulting Area (males and females)

Male and female gymnasts run along a runway towards a springboard, which helps them leap up and over the vault table.

The Balance Beam (females only)

The balance beam is for females only. They perform balances, jumps, leaps and running steps along the 10cm wide top of the beam.

The Uneven Bars (females only)

These are used by females only, to perform similar skills to those done by men on the horizontal bar. There are two bars, so the routines can be very spectacular (see pages 16-17).

(From top left) The balance beam, the pommel horse, the rings and the vaulting table are just some of the apparatus that gymnasts use to perform on.

9

The Floor

Floor routines involve a combination of stunning tumbling sequences with skilful balances, twists and other manoeuvres.

The Floor Area

Floor routines are performed on a padded mat, inside an area measuring 12.2m square. Male and female gymnasts use the same size floor area. The padded area continues outside the square for safety, but if the gymnasts step or tumble outside the square accidentally, they lose points.

Handstand to High Forward Roll

1 *First, the gymnast steps well forward to begin a handstand. From a strong starting position like this, she will be able to do a kick up that will leave her standing on her hands in balance.*

2 *Now the gymnast is in balance in the handstand: notice that her body and legs form a straight line. This is an ideal handstand: a curved back or legs that do not stick straight up will lose points.*

3 *Next the gymnast rolls her head forwards and lets her arms bend. Her legs stay straight up in the air, and she rolls downwards on a curved back.*

Routines

The biggest feature of male gymnasts' floor routines is spectacular tumbling sequences, though other skills are also used. The routines have to show that the gymnast is flexible, strong and has good balance. He is expected to use each of the four corners of the floor at least once during the routine.

Unlike male floor exercises, female floor routines are set to vocal-free music. Their routines are choreographed, which means that they include some dance skills, as well as tumbles and balance skills.

Backflips can make up a spectacular part of floor routines, especially when peformed at speed.

Even just a corner of a heel touching the boundary will result in lost points if the judges spot it.

4 **5** The gymnast bends her knees just as her bottom hits the floor, using the momentum of the roll to stand up.

6 The gymnast stands up straight, arms above head and ready to perform the next skill. The best floor exercises link lots of different skills smoothly together.

11

Vaulting

Vaulting is one of the oldest gymnastics events. It has its roots in ancient Greece, where young men leapt over charging bulls to prove their bravery.

Modern-day Vaulting

Despite the lack of charging bulls, modern-day vaulting still requires bravery. It can be dangerous, so it is important to learn the techniques only with a qualified coach.

The Handspring

1 *Gymnasts keep the same long, slightly arched body shape all the way through a handspring. To do this, they need a reasonably fast run-up.*

Judging speed on the runway is an important part of vaulting. Not enough speed and the vault will be impossible to complete properly. Too much and it will be wild and uncontrolled.

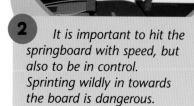

2 *It is important to hit the springboard with speed, but also to be in control. Sprinting wildly in towards the board is dangerous.*

3 *As she leaps towards the vaulting table, the gymnast reaches up and forwards. It's important to keep looking ahead to where your hands will be placed.*

4 *Once her hands are firmly planted on the table, the thrust stage of the vault begins. The gymnast keeps her head still, and tightens her bottom muscles to help her legs come over.*

The Stages of a Vault

Each vault is made up of seven crucial stages:

- The run-up.
- A hurdle step, which allows the vaulter to change from running to a two-footed landing on the springboard.
- The jump from the springboard.
- First flight, towards the vaulting table.
- The thrust, or pushing, stage, when the vaulter comes into contact with the vaulting table.
- Second flight, when the vaulter leaves the table.

- Landing, when vaulters bend their legs to absorb the force of the landing. They land flat on their feet, with their feet pointing slightly outwards.

The Handspring

This is one of the most commonly performed vaults, and also the one that is most often performed badly. Gymnasts can avoid developing bad habits by learning on a low-set vaulting table, then increasing the height of the table once their technique is perfect.

The springboard helps convert runway speed into upwards motion.

5   *During the second flight stage of the vault, the gymnast aims to keeps her body in an arched shape and let her head drop back a little. This helps to keep enough rotation in the vault.*

6   7   *As her feet land, the gymnast bends her knees to absorb the shock. Her arms are opened out to the side for balance. She then stands up straight, arms in the air, to finish the vault.*

The Balance Beam

At the top level of competition, only female gymnasts perform on the balance beam. It is the most difficult piece of apparatus and even a small mistake can – and often does – lead to a fall.

5m long, and just 10cm wide. Despite the beam being only just a little wider than most people's feet, top gymnasts perform leaps, twists and tumbling sequences along it.

Routines are divided into:
- A mount.
- A sequence of moves on the beam, which will include simple dance steps, leaps, rolls and jumps. Advanced gymnasts are even able to add some floor skills (such as back flips) to their beam routines.
- A dismount.

Balance-beam Routines

Balance-beam routines are performed on a lightly padded strip of wood, 1.25m above the ground,

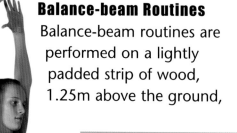

A Forward Roll on the Beam

1 *The gymnast starts in a balanced position, with one foot in front of the other.*

2 *From there, she crouches smoothly, keeping a straight back for good shape.*

3 *Rolling forwards, the gymnast grips the beam as she tucks her head into the roll and pushes off her front foot.*

Learning Balance-beam Skills

If everyone who wanted to learn the balance beam had to start off 1.25m above the ground, the queue of people waiting to have a go would probably be very short. Fortunately, beam skills can be developed on the floor. Gymnasts start by practising their skills on a line along the floor or on a wide bench. Next they move to a low beam, before finally testing their skills on a competition beam.

Olga Korbut

Date of birth: May 16th, 1955

Nationality: born in Belarus, now a U.S. citizen

At one time, Olga Korbut was the world's most famous gymnast. When she was just fourteen, she wowed the world with two new gymnastics moves. The first was a backwards aerial somersault on the balance beam. The skill immediately became known as a 'Korbut salto'. The second was a backflip-to-catch on the uneven bars, or 'Korbut flip'. Olga went on to great success in gymnastics:

- Three gold medals at the 1972 Munich Olympics.
- Five medals at the 1974 World Gymnastics Championships.
- A fourth Olympic gold medal at the 1976 Montreal Olympics.

4 *If the roll has been straight and the gymnast has kept her feet together, her feet will hit the beam as she rolls forwards.*

5 *The gymnast's arms are forward to help her continue the movement back to a standing position.*

The Bars

Bar work is probably the most spectacular gymnastic event. The competitors show great bravery as they pick up speed by swinging around and around a thin bar high in the air.

The Horizontal Bar

Men's bar work is done using a single bar. In competition, the bar is 2.75m above the ground. Fortunately for beginners, most coaches start their students off on a bar about shoulder high. Each complete spin around the bar is called a *giant*. After building up speed with a succession of giants, advanced gymnasts let go of the bar and launch spectacular moves. They then either catch the bar and continue their routine, or dismount.

The Uneven Bars

Women compete on uneven or 'asymmetric' bars, one higher than the other. The bars are 2.46m and 1.66m above the ground. The gymnast swings around each bar, switching between the two in the blink of an eye.

Young female gymnasts train using just one of the asymmetric bars and move on to using both bars as they get stronger and more skilled.

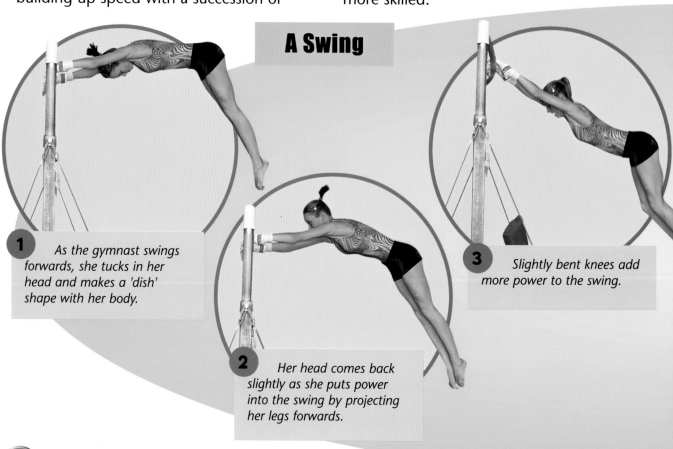

A Swing

1 As the gymnast swings forwards, she tucks in her head and makes a 'dish' shape with her body.

2 Her head comes back slightly as she puts power into the swing by projecting her legs forwards.

3 Slightly bent knees add more power to the swing.

Beth Tweddle

Date of birth: April 1st, 1985

Nationality: British

Beth started gymnastics classes when she was seven years old. She has become the most successful British gymnast ever. Beth's best event is the asymmetric bars, but she is an all-rounder, so much so that she won the title of British All-Round Champion every year from 2001 to 2005. She is the first British gymnast to win medals on the world gymnastics stage, including:

• Bronze medals at the 2003 and 2005 World Championships.

• Gold on the asymmetric bars at the 2006 European Championships.

• Gold on the asymmetric bars at the 2006 World Championships.

Beth Tweddle performs on the bars at the 2006 British ladies' gymnastics championships. ▶

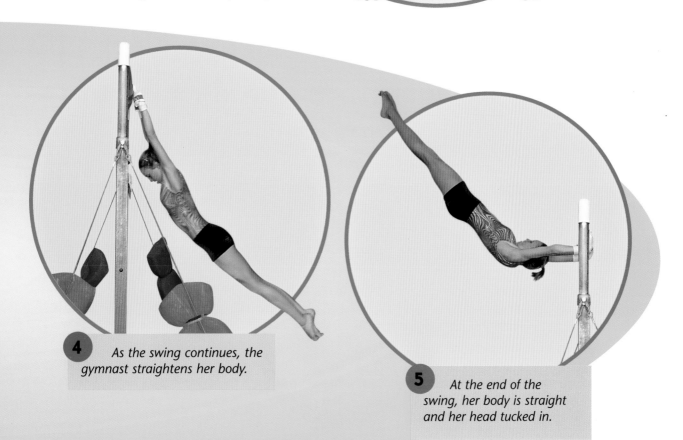

4 *As the swing continues, the gymnast straightens her body.*

5 *At the end of the swing, her body is straight and her head tucked in.*

The Parallel Bars

The parallel bars are used only by male gymnasts. The skills they use are mainly swinging, and the judges look for smooth swinging and flight of the body between moves.

The Equipment

Parallel bars are made up of two wooden or plastic bars 195cm above the ground, 350cm long and with a gap of 42-52cm between them. Underneath there is padding, in case the gymnast slips or falls.

The Swing

The swing is the crucial skill in parallel-bar work, and the first, most important thing young gymnasts learn. It works like a pendulum, with the gymnast's shoulders moving forwards as his feet go backwards.

The Upstart on Parallel Bars

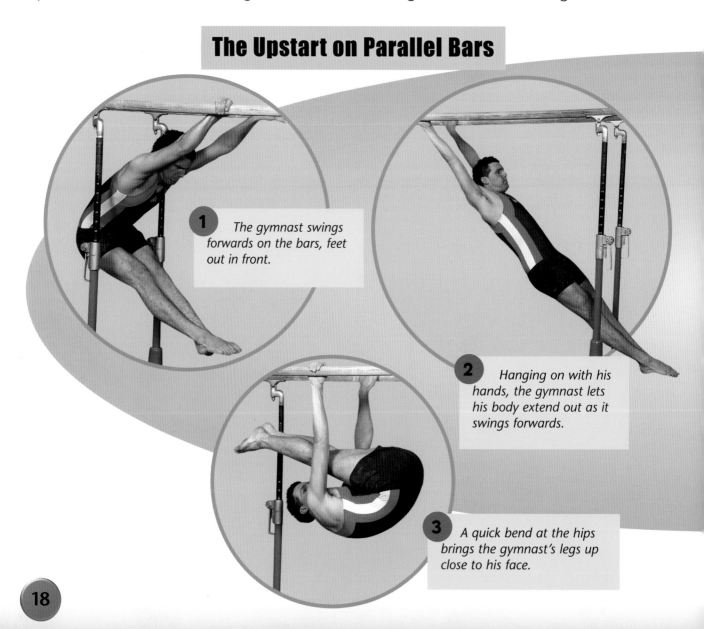

1 The gymnast swings forwards on the bars, feet out in front.

2 Hanging on with his hands, the gymnast lets his body extend out as it swings forwards.

3 A quick bend at the hips brings the gymnast's legs up close to his face.

The swing begins from the shoulders and chest. The gymnast's body is held straight, but a slight kick of his feet at the end of the forward swing helps keep the swing going.

The swing can be done while the gymnast is resting on his hands, from a hanging position, and from an upper-arm position.

The Upstart

This allows a gymnast to get into a raised position on the bars, resting on his hands. The upwards thrust happens during the second part of the movement, and has to be timed carefully with the pendulum movement of the gymnast's swing.

The Routine

A typical routine on the bars usually includes:
• Swinging skills.
• Flips and turns, where the gymnast changes direction or spins around.
• Strength positions, where the gymnast holds a difficult shape without moving.
• A dismount, in which the gymnast swings off the bars and finishes the routine standing beside them.

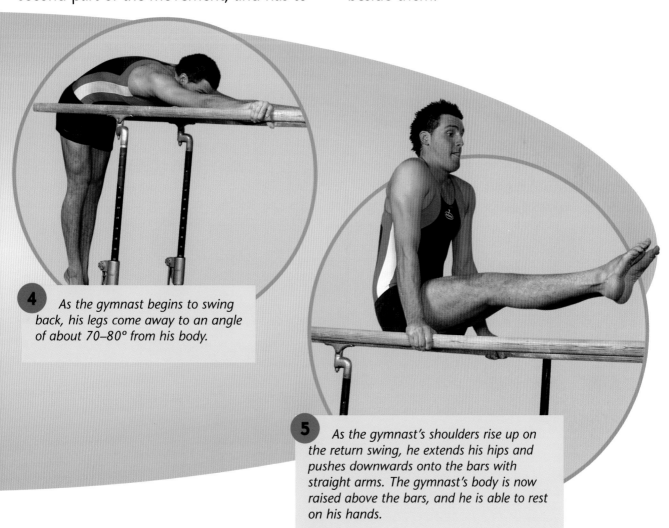

4 *As the gymnast begins to swing back, his legs come away to an angle of about 70–80° from his body.*

5 *As the gymnast's shoulders rise up on the return swing, he extends his hips and pushes downwards onto the bars with straight arms. The gymnast's body is now raised above the bars, and he is able to rest on his hands.*

The Pommel Horse and Rings

As with the parallel bars, only male gymnasts compete on the pommel horse and rings. These pieces of apparatus require a combination of technique and, especially for the most spectacular moves, strength.

The Pommel Horse

On the pommel horse, gymnasts swing their legs around and around the horse, supporting themselves on their hands.
As they swing around, they perform a series of manoeuvres with their legs, including:

* Double leg circles, where the gymnast's legs are held together as he pivots round and round on the pommels.
* Flares, where the gymnast's outside leg is pointed straight into the air as his lower leg passes the pommel.

* Scissors, where the gymnast pivots to and fro on the pommels, lifting and dropping his legs on either side of the horse in a scissors movement.
* A handstand leading to dismount.

The Rings

On the rings, gymnasts perform a combination of swings and strength moves. Strength moves are motionless positions that require good balance and control of the rings. One of the most famous is the crucifix, where the gymnast holds his arms straight out to the sides and hangs still, with legs pointing straight downwards.

A Smooth Swing

A smooth swing is crucial for the rings. Without it, it will be impossible to stop the rings swaying. Keeping downwards pressure on the rings all the time helps keep the swing smooth.

A gymnast lifts his arm from the pommel to let his legs swing past.

Swinging on the Rings

1 *The gymnast swings forwards with arms and legs fully extended.*

2 *As the gymnast's weight comes forward, he tenses his body and legs from the hips, and keeps downward force on the rings. This tensing adds momentum to the swing.*

3 *The gymnast comes towards the top of the swing. He keeps tension on the rings, which have moved outwards slightly as his body rose up.*

4 *As the gymnast comes through the top of his swing, he relaxes his body.*

5 *The gymnast swings down and back towards his starting position, ready for another smooth swing.*

Rhythmic Gymnastics

Rhythmic gymnastics is mainly for female gymnasts, although it is increasingly popular with male gymnasts in a few countries, especially in Asia. It combines gymnastic and dance skills.

- A rubber or plastic ball, about 20cm across.
- Clubs, which look similar to jugglers' clubs.
- A wooden or plastic hoop, about 85cm across.
- A long ribbon on the end of a short stick.
- A rope with a knot at each end.

Equipment

In rhythmic gymnastics, competitors use additional pieces of equipment as part of their routine. These are:

Building a Routine

Only one piece of equipment is used in each routine. The equipment is a crucial part of the combination of dance and gymnastics skills.

▼ This gymnast is integrating artistic use of the ribbon with her gymnastic skills

Ribbon
The ribbon is long and light, and can be thrown or waved to make designs in the air around the gymnast. The designs include snakes, spirals and loops.

Hoop
The hoop creates a space for the gymnast to use. Her routine includes movements through the hoop – for example, forward rolls.

Ball
Routines using a ball combine spectacular throws and catches with gymnastic movements.

Rope
The rope can be held taught or loose, in one hand or two. It winds and unwinds around the gymnast like a serpent.

Clubs
Gymnasts use the clubs for asymmetric movements, rolling, twisting, throwing and catching them first with one arm then the other.

A team from Spain dances in the rhythmic gymnastics group qualifications during the 2004 Summer Olympic Games in Athens.

Types of Contest

There are different types of contest for rhythmic gymnastics:

- In individual contests, the gymnasts must use four of the five pieces of equipment.
- In team contests, members of five-person teams split the five pieces of equipment between them.

Rhythmic gymnastics was first included in the World Gymnastics Championships in 1963. The sport has been part of the Olympics since the 1984 Los Angeles Olympics.

Scoring

In 2005, a new system of scoring was introduced. Each routine is now given a score of up to 20 points. The score is based on three elements of the gymnast's routine:

- Technical difficulty.
- Artistic elements.
- How well the skills have been done.

The aim of the new system was to reward gymnasts with good technical skills.

Men's Rhythmic Gymnastics

Men's rhythmic gymnastics is particularly popular in Asia, especially in Japan. There, the sport combines rhythmic gymnastics, artistic gymnastics and wushu martial arts. No ball is used, and routines include tumbling.

Trampolining

Anyone who has tried trampolining in a friend's garden knows what fun it can be. Trampolining is part of the world of gymnastics.

The First Trampolines

A man called George Nissen made the first trampolines in the 1930s. He based his invention on the safety nets used by circus trapeze artists. The principles of the trampoline have been the same ever since: a flexible, bouncy mat with springs around the edges, which allows you to bounce up and down to a great height.

Modern Equipment

Modern competition trampolines measure 4.3m by 2.1m. Around the edges of the trampoline are thick, padded mats called safety platforms. A cross marks the centre of the trampoline. Trampolinists aim to land as near as possible to this cross for each bounce. Too far away, and they will lose points from their score.

Safe Training

During training, trampolinists sometimes wear a spotting belt. This is a belt that is attached to overhead pulleys. It allows the coach to stop the trampolinist falling dangerously.

Competitions

In 2000, trampolining became one of the Olympic gymnastics disciplines. During their routines, the trampolinists perform a series of skills including single, double or even triple somersaults and twists. They must start and finish each routine on their feet,

The different landing positions used in trampolining: (top left) landing 'to feet'; (bottom left) landing 'to seat' (in a sitting-down position with the legs straight ahead); (top right) landing 'to front', with the hands under the chin; and (bottom right) landing 'to back' (on your back with arms and legs pointing upwards).

The three basic body shapes used during a trampolining routine: (top left) the tuck; (top right) the pike; and (left) straight.

From the Spanish

The word 'trampoline' comes from the Spanish word *trampolin*, which means 'diving board'.

and aim to hold their body shape throughout each skill. There are two types of competition: individual and synchronised.

Individual Contests

Trampolinists perform two routines, each with 10 skills. In the compulsory routine, four of the skills are required by the regulations. The trampolinist chooses the other six. In the voluntary routine, the trampolinist gets to choose all 10 skills.

Synchronised Contests

In synchronised contests, two trampolinists on side-by-side trampolines perform the exact same routine. They aim to stay in perfect time with each other, with each looking like a mirror image of the other.

Jason Burnett

Date of birth: December 16th, 1986

Nationality: Canadian

Jason Burnett specialises in high-difficulty routines on the trampoline. This has allowed him to become the highest-scoring trampolinist ever. The previous highest-score record had been 17.0 points, a record held jointly by Igor Gelimbatovsky (USSR) and Daniel Neale (GB).

Rumours that Burnett had performed an amazing 18.5 points in training were confirmed in competition in 2007. He managed a 17.5-point routine, breaking the world record highest score in the process.

25

Competitions

Gymnastics competitions are run at every level, from local club championships to the Olympics and world championships. Whatever the event, every gymnast aims to improve his or her personal best score.

Olympics and World Championships

The Olympics and world championships are the toughest competitions in the world of gymnastics. The Olympics, which only comes around every four years, is the one almost every gymnast has dreamed of winning.

The gymnasts at the Olympics and world championships are entered as national teams of six. The competition is divided into four parts: team qualifying, team finals, all-round finals, and event finals:

- Team qualifying: up to five of the six gymnasts in each team compete on each apparatus. The best four of their scores are counted towards the team total. (This is called the '6-5-4 format'.)

Young gymnasts take part in local competitions.

Team managers and coaches help the gymnasts, making sure they are ready for their events.

- Team finals: the top eight teams from the qualifying session compete, but this time only three of the six gymnasts can compete on each piece of apparatus. All three scores count.
- All-round finals: the top 24 gymnasts from the team qualifying session qualify for the all-round finals. Only two gymnasts per country are allowed.
- Event finals: these are competitions for the top eight gymnasts for each piece of apparatus. Only two gymnasts from each country can qualify for each apparatus.

The World Cup and Other Competitions

The World Cup is a series of major gymnastics competitions that takes place around the world every year. These and other competitions do not always work in the same way as the Olympics. In the World Cup, for example, there are no team competitions at all. Only individual all-round and apparatus contests take place.

Nadia Comaneci

Date of birth: November 12th, 1961

Nationality: born in Romania, now lives in the USA

Nadia Comaneci arrived at the 1976 Olympics as a tiny, 4' 11", 86lb 14-year-old. No one really expected her to win anything. But Comaneci's performance on the asymmetric bars took the gymnastics world by storm: she scored the first-ever perfect 10 at the Olympics. Not content with that, she scored six more through the rest of the competition. Her other achievements include:

- Three gold medals at the 1976 Olympics.

- Two further golds at the 1980 Moscow Olympics.

- Gold medals at the 1978 and 1979 world championships.

Nadia Comaneci performing at the Montreal Olympics in 1976, when she was just 14 years old

Record Holders

Most Men's Olympic Medals

• Nikolay Andrianov (USSR) won a record 15 Olympic medals (seven gold, five silver, and three bronze) from 1972 to 1980.

• Aleksandr Dityatin (USSR) won a record eight medals at one Olympic Games, in Moscow, Russia (then USSR), in 1980. He won three gold, four silver and one bronze.

Most Men's Olympic Titles

• The men's team title has been won five times by Japan (1960, 1964, 1968, 1972 and 1976) and the USSR (1952, 1956, 1980, 1988 and 1992).

• Two gymnasts have won six men's individual gold medals, the biggest number ever: Boris Shakhlin (USSR) won one in 1956, four (two shared) in 1960, and one in 1964; Nikolay Andrianov (USSR) won one in 1972, four in 1976, and one in 1980.

Most Women's Olympic Titles

• The USSR won the Olympic women's title a record 10 times (from 1952 to 1980, and in 1988 and 1992). The last title was won by a Unified Team from the republics of the former USSR.

• Vera Caslavska-Odlozil (Czechoslovakia) holds the record for the most individual gold medals: three in 1964 and four (one shared) in 1968.

Most Women's Medals

• Larisa Latynina (USSR) won six individual gold medals and three team golds from 1956 to 1964. She also won five silver and four bronze medals, making an Olympic-record total of 18.

Glossary

Apparatus A piece of equipment designed for a special purpose. In gymnastics, competitions take place on one of seven possible pieces of apparatus: floor, vaulting table, rings, pommel horse, parallel bars, asymmetric bars and beam.

Asymmetric Not equal or the same on both sides. In the asymmetric bars, for example, one bar is higher than the other.

Average The middle of a group of scores or numbers. One way of finding an average is to add up all the scores, then divide them by the number of scores. So, for example, if three judges score a gymnast 7.85, 8.20 and 8.35, the average would be (7.85 + 8.20 + 8.35) ÷ 3, which is 8.13.

Czechoslovakia Former country in central Europe, which divided into the Czech

Republic and the Slovak Republic on 1 January 1993.

Dismount In gymnastics, the process of getting off a piece of apparatus such as a pommel horse to end the routine.

Flight Movement through the air.

Martial arts Styles of fighting, for example taekwondo or judo.

Momentum Forwards movement, especially at an increasing speed.

Paralysis Not being able to move. In humans, paralysis is usually caused by damage to the spine.

Pharaohs The rulers of ancient Egypt.

Pommel The curved handle that is attached at both ends to the top of a pommel horse.

Rotation A turning or spinning motion.

Specialists In gymnastics, specialists are people who usually compete on a particular piece of apparatus.

Trapeze A horizontal bar attached at each end to a rope. In circuses, gymnastic tricks by people swinging from the trapeze are always a popular attraction.

Troupes Groups of performers.

USSR Short for the Union of Soviet Socialist Republics, a country that existed from 1922 to 1991. It then split into many new countries, of which the largest and most powerful is Russia.

Vocal Using the voice, especially for singing.

Wushu Chinese martial arts.

Websites

www.british-gymnastics.org

The home website of British Gymnastics, with news about the British team, latest competitions, results, information about technique and coaching, and help in finding a gymnastics club near you.

www.olympic.org

The official website of the Olympic Movement, with a section that deals with gymnastics. Profiles of famous Olympic gymnasts, plus information about the different gymnastics disciplines.

www.fig-gymnastics.org

The home site of the FIG (the Fédération Internationale de Gymnastique), the world governing body for gymnastics, this is the place to find out about rules, clothing and results from world events.

http://tinyurl.com/ysul2s

Free online, animated tutorials for basic gymnastics techniques, plus advice on correcting errors in your technique.

Index